GETTING TO KNOW

JUN 2 5 2019

Minecraft

ADAM FURGANG

rosen publishing's
rosen central

New York

Published in 2019 by The Rosen Publishing Group, Inc.
29 East 21st Street, New York, NY 10010

First Edition

Library of Congress Cataloging-in-Publication Data

Names: Furgang, Adam, author.
Title: Getting to know Minecraft / Adam Furgang.
Description: First edition. | New York : Rosen Publishing, 2019. | Series: Code power : a teen programmer's guide | Includes bibliographical references and index. | Audience: Grades 5–8.
Identifiers: LCCN 2018018358 | ISBN 9781508183792 (library bound) | ISBN 9781508183785 (pbk.)
Subjects: LCSH: Minecraft (Game)—Juvenile literature. | Computer games—Programming—Juvenile literature. | Simulation games in education—Juvenile literature.
Classification: LCC GV1469.35.M535 F87 2019 | DDC 794.8—dc23
LC record available at https://lccn.loc.gov/2018018358

Manufactured in the United States of America

{ CONTENTS

INTRODUCTION 4

CHAPTER 1
HOW TO PLAY THE
ULTIMATE SANDBOX
GAME
8

CHAPTER 2
SET UP FOR MODDING
MINECRAFT
18

CHAPTER 3
COMPUTERCRAFT AND
BEYOND
30

CHAPTER 4
THE COMPUTER
LANGUAGE BEHIND
MINECRAFT
39

CHAPTER 5
MINECRAFT AS
EDUCATION
45

GLOSSARY 52
FOR MORE INFORMATION 54
FOR FURTHER READING 57
BIBLIOGRAPHY 59
INDEX 62

E veryone knows what *Minecraft* is. It is one of the most popular video games in history. To date, *Minecraft* has sold more than 144 million copies and is now the second best-selling video game of all time, just behind the popular puzzle video game Tetris. *Minecraft* also had 74 million active players in 2017.

Minecraft is not just a typical video game. *Minecraft* is a creation-focused, exploration-based video game that takes place within a three-dimensional environment, and it bridges the gap between a playable game and a programmable software language. Not only can players build within *Minecraft* but they can also mod (short for modify) the game world by entering various strings of computer software code commands. Changing parts of the computer code allows players to change various aspects of the game, such as difficulty, game modes, and the look and feel of the *Minecraft* world.

Unlike most video games—which must be played with a specific set of rules and objectives—*Minecraft* allows players to do whatever they want. The world of *Minecraft* is made up of cubes of raw materials, such as wood, stone, dirt, and other various ores and minerals. Players can hack away at the landscape with tools they find in the environment, such as swords, pick axes, and shovels. Players use the tools to dig, explore, build, and manipulate the *Minecraft* landscape any way they choose. Players can also build and create items and buildings from scratch using tools and materials they acquire as they explore.

Swedish video game programmer Markus Persson, nicknamed Notch, independently created *Minecraft*. Persson learned to write computer code on a Commodore 128 computer his father

>> Kids and adults play *Minecraft* side by side at a Microsoft store opening in New York City in 2015.

brought home, and he began creating simple video games by the time he was eight. Persson knew from a young age that he wanted to create video games and started working at his first software programming job when he was just eighteen.

In addition to this programming job, Persson began developing video games for himself and his friends. *Minecraft* was Persson's first independently created video game, and he released it to the public on May 17, 2009, for a low price. Shortly after its release, *Minecraft* became a massive success, and by 2012, Perssonn's company, Mojang, was earning $230 million in sales. In 2014, Persson sold Mojang, along with *Minecraft*, to Microsoft for $2.5 billion. Since Microsoft acquired Mojang, successive updates

>> *Minecraft* cubes have an iconic, bricklike appearance; players either build up or break down the game with pickaxes and other tools.

and editions of *Minecraft* have been released on multiple gaming platforms and purchased by 100 million people. Today players can play and modify *Minecraft* on personal computers, game consoles, and even on mobile devices such as smartphones and tablets.

Being able to modify parts of the *Minecraft* code has introduced countless players to Java, the software language in which *Minecraft* was originally written. For a player to make changes within *Minecraft*, he or she will need to write some simple Java computer code—or copy lines of code others have written—and add them into the game. This book will introduce *Minecraft* players to the computer programming language Java and will show other ways to get started modifying *Minecraft* on various gaming platforms.

CHAPTER 1

HOW TO PLAY THE ULTIMATE SANDBOX GAME

Many popular video games are made by big companies and require large budgets with millions of dollars and dozens—or even hundreds—of people to create. The Disney video game *Epic Mickey 2*, for example, had seven hundred people working to

>> In 2012, *Minecraft* creator and Swedish computer programmer Markus Persson, referred to as Notch, received the Special Award at the British Academy Video Games Awards ceremony in London.

create it. Other popular video games were created by teams that total more than a thousand people working at studios in different locations around the world. So it may be surprising to learn that one of the most popular video games of all time, *Minecraft*, was created by just one person: Markus "Notch" Persson.

WHAT IS *MINECRAFT* AND HOW TO PLAY

Minecraft is an open world, or sandbox style, game. A sandbox game puts few restrictions on the player, who is allowed to roam freely within the game environment. The various landscapes in *Minecraft* are called biomes.

Different biomes have different geographical features, such as deserts and forests. Players can download various maps and texture packs (also called resource packs) and use them to change up the look and feel of the game. Players in *Minecraft* can break apart the landscape and obtain playing pieces called blocks. Blocks can be used to craft tools, buildings, or anything else players can imagine.

>> After Microsoft purchased Mojang in 2014, it released its own versions of *Minecraft* for different consoles; the Mojang logo still appears on every box.

The game also contains mobs, which is short for "mobiles." Mobs are animals, such as chickens, pigs, or horses. They can also be monsters, such as zombies or spiders, or creatures unique to the *Minecraft* world called creepers. Some of the hardest mobs to defeat are called boss mobs, such as the Ender Dragon or the Wither.

The most complete and programmable version of *Minecraft* can be played on a personal computer by using an online account with Mojang. *Minecraft* can also be purchased and played on various gaming consoles such as PlayStation, Xbox, Nintendo Switch, and various mobile devices, such as Android and Apple smartphones. Some aspects of gameplay and controls, and the ability to mod *Minecraft*, can vary from system to system, but the basics of the game are always the same.

>>MARKUS "NOTCH" PERSSON

Markus "Notch" Persson was born in Stockholm, Sweden, on June 1, 1979. His nickname, Notch, is also his internet handle, or nickname. Persson grew up in the remote town of Edsbyn, Sweden, surrounded by woods. As a child, he loved playing with the plastic building toy LEGO. He fondly recalls his time playing outdoors and exploring the woods, an experience he says helped influence his creation of *Minecraft*. Another big influence came when Persson was just seven years old. One day, his father, Birger, brought home a Commodore 128 computer. Persson fell in love with the computer and created his first computer program by the time he was eight years old.

Persson did not finish high school, but he took a course in which he learned the computer programming language C++ and started his first job as a computer programmer when he was just eighteen. After working at different jobs programming and creating small video games for the industry, Persson decided to

(continued on the next page)

```
#include <cmath>

// computes the factorial
// of the given number
int factorial(int input_number) {
    if(input_number == 0) {
        // always check for zero input and retur
        return 1;
    }
    // to get the factorial find the factorial of a
    return(input_number * factorial(input_number -
}
// computes the nth power of the given number called va
int power(int value, int power) {
    if(power == 0) {
        return 1;
    }
    return(value * power(value, power - 1));
}


    std::cin >> ch;
    if(ch != 'w') {
        ++depth;
        get_input(ch);
    }
    else {
        std::cout << "depth:= " << depth << std
    }
    return depth;
}

int main() {
    _reverse("hello world!");
    return 0;
}
```

>> After leaving high school, Markus Persson took a course on writing the C++ programming language. This was his basis as he started programming *Minecraft* in Java.

(continued from the previous page)

make a video game of his own in his spare time. He released *Minecraft* to the public on May 17, 2009.

By the summer of 2010, gamers had purchased 20,000 copies of *Minecraft*, and Persson was able to quit his programming job to work on *Minecraft* full-time. His close friend Jakob Porser agreed to work with him. Soon the two men started the company Mojang, which is the Swedish word for gadget. By 2012, Mojang had earned $230 million in sales. In 2014, Persson sold *Minecraft*, along with Mojang, to Microsoft for $2.5 billion.

GAMEPLAY

Minecraft has several different game modes, yet there are no instructions on how to play or what to do, and there are no set goals for players. Despite this unconventional setup, *Minecraft* has become one of the most popular video games of all time.

When a game of *Minecraft* begins, a player starts with no tools or possessions. There are five different game modes in *Minecraft*: survival, creative, adventure, hardcore, and spectator. A player will have to decide before starting a game if he or she wants the option of being able to switch between these game modes so a special cheat option can be switched on. Players can also choose to play as a single player or to play online in the same mode with a group of players.

SURVIVAL MODE

One of the most popular game modes in *Minecraft* is survival mode. In this mode, players must collect supplies, craft tools, build shelter, battle monsters, get food, and explore the landscape in an effort to stay alive and continue to play.

When a player chooses to play in survival mode, gameplay becomes dangerous once the sun sets over the landscape. At night in *Minecraft*, various monsters—including skeletons, zombies, spiders, and creepers—emerge. Creepers, perhaps the most famous of all the *Minecraft* monsters, are colored green and will explode if they get too close to a player. A player can be killed in survival mode by the various threats that exist throughout the *Minecraft* world.

CREATIVE MODE

In creative mode, players do not need to worry about the dangers they face in survival mode. They can't die; are not hungry; and have more freedom to explore, build, and create. Players can even fly in creative mode, and they move around freely. Players have complete access to an infinite amount of all raw materials and items. They can also easily destroy all blocks to tunnel through the ground and alter the landscape with no difficulty.

What can a player do in creative mode? The goal of creative mode is simply to be creative. Players can design maps; test new updates; build giant homes, buildings, or structures; and create massive freestanding or floating art pieces by using the different colored blocks as pixels. The possibilities of what can be done in creative mode are infinite.

ADVENTURE MODE

In adventure mode, players have the ability to showcase maps, structures, and predetermined adventures they build while in creative mode. New players can enter another carefully constructed world in adventure mode and interact with it in a limited way without having the ability to destroy it. Blocks and other items cannot be broken in adventure mode. Many players use adventure mode to explore role-playing and adventure games with friends.

HARDCORE MODE

As its name implies, this is a very difficult version of survival mode. The modes are the same except for one major difference: when a player dies in hardcore mode, they cannot respawn, or come back to life. Respawning is an important way for players to continue to build or explore in other modes, but hardcore is meant to be punishing if played carelessly.

SPECTATOR MODE

This mode allows players to observe the world of *Minecraft* in a very unique way. Watching other people play *Minecraft* has become very popular, and that is what this mode allows. Gamers in spectator mode can fly around and move through solid objects to see and observe everything going on within the *Minecraft* world. They can even see things from the perspective of monsters and animals. Players in spectator mode cannot break or interact with anything within the world. A player in spectator mode can watch a *Minecraft* game being played in survival, creative, or adventure modes.

>>FROM LEGO TO *MINECRAFT* TO LEGO

The blocklike structure of LEGO bricks are so similar to *Minecraft* bricks and mods that it is hard to imagine a time when *Minecraft* LEGO sets did not exist.

Before Lego and Mojang teamed up, Markus Persson spoke about LEGO in an interview with *ToyNews*: "Having grown up with LEGO and it probably having subconsciously affected the design of *Minecraft*—I'd say it's a perfect match."

Eventually, LEGO and Mojang did team up, and the first small *Minecraft*-themed LEGO set was available for purchase

(continued on the next page)

>> It is not by chance that LEGOs and *Minecraft* look very similar. Markus Persson loved playing and building with LEGO bricks as a child, and they helped inspire him to make *Minecraft*.

(continued from the previous page)

in the summer of 2012. Several more sets were released. By 2014, a partnership was announced, along with the release of six new sets. The largest LEGO *Minecraft* set was the Mountain Cave set. The set measures 12 inches high by 20 inches wide by 11 inches deep (30 centimeters by 51 cm by 28 cm) and has 2,863 pieces of LEGO with which to build.

WHAT IS COMPUTER SOFTWARE?

Computers, video games (including *Minecraft*), programs, apps, and many electronic devices rely on computer programs to run. Computer programs are commands written out in various software languages, which direct a computer to perform certain processes in a certain order. Computer programmers use different types of software languages to create computer programs or video games.

There are various types of software, such as system software and application software. System software is a program used as a computer's operating system that tells the computer what to do and how to operate. Other types of software, such as application software, can be installed within a computer's operating system. Some types of application software are word processing software, database software, internet browsers, and game software.

When Markus Persson created *Minecraft*, he used the software programming language called Java. Java is one of the most popular programming languages in the world. Spoken languages, such as English or Spanish, have specific rules in order to speak and write with them. Computer software languages have their own specific rules, too. These rules allow computers running the languages to carry out specific commands. A video game like *Minecraft* is made up of thousands of lines of Java computer code, which combine to tell the computer how to run the game. The ways a game looks, sounds, and behaves are all determined by the software code that was written by a person called a programmer.

Below is a short piece of Java code from the book *Minecraft Modding with Forge: A Family-Friendly Guide to Building Fun Mods in Java*:

```
public class
BlockBreakMessage
{
                @SubscribeEvent
                public void sendMessage(BreakEvent event) {
                        event.getPlayer().addChatMessage(
                                new
            ChatComponentText(EnumChatFormatting.GOLD
                                        + "You broke a
        block!"));
                }
        }
```

Although the code may look complicated—after all, it is a foreign language—it is easy to learn how to read with the right training.

CHAPTER 2

SET UP FOR MODDING *MINECRAFT*

Aside from just playing *Minecraft*, it is also possible to alter the gameplay with mods. Since its initial release in 2009, both Mojang and Microsoft have continued to update *Minecraft*, and additional updates continue to this day. There have also

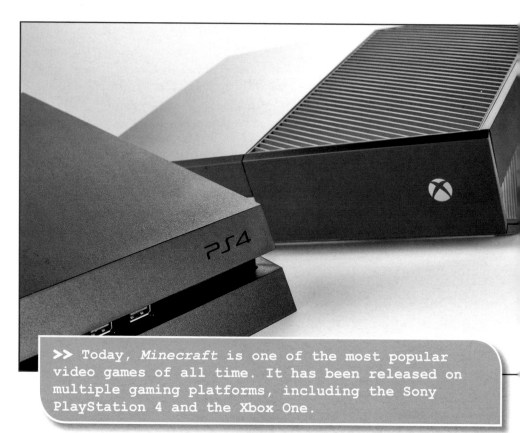

>> Today, *Minecraft* is one of the most popular video games of all time. It has been released on multiple gaming platforms, including the Sony PlayStation 4 and the Xbox One.

been many different versions and editions of *Minecraft*. Initially, *Minecraft* was released for personal computers, both Windows and Macintosh. As *Minecraft* became more popular, various editions were released on different gaming consoles, including the Xbox and PlayStation. The Pocket edition of *Minecraft* was released in 2011 on various mobile devices. Each edition of *Minecraft* is slightly different, and not every version supports mods. The common thread between all versions, however, is support for some level of customization.

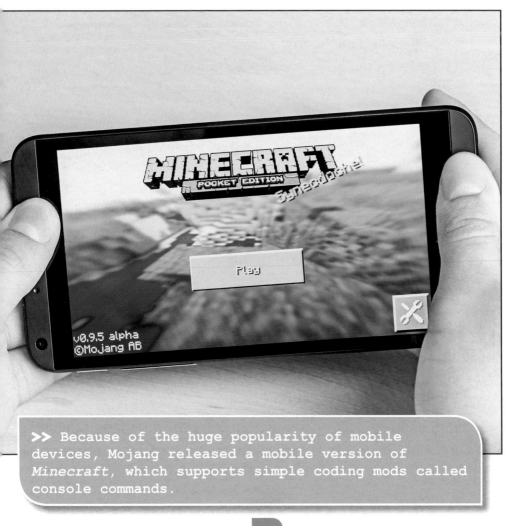

>> Because of the huge popularity of mobile devices, Mojang released a mobile version of *Minecraft*, which supports simple coding mods called console commands.

WAYS TO MODIFY *MINECRAFT* WITHOUT CODING

Minecraft on console gaming platforms such as Xbox and PlayStation does not support player-created Java mods. Players of *Minecraft* on console systems will still be able to change certain limited aspects of the game with official additional paid content that can be downloaded.

- **Texture packs** change the look of the objects throughout the world.
- **Skin packs** change the outfits of the various playable and nonplayable characters.
- **Mash-up packs** apply modifications to the title screen and come with a skin pack, a texture pack, and a themed world.

The themes for all packs are generally taken from different popular films, television shows, and game properties. Theme packs are available for *Stranger Things, Adventure Time*, and the card game Magic: The Gathering. Some themes are only available on certain systems. For example, the *LittleBigPlanet* Mash-up Pack is only available on PlayStation, and the *Halo* Mash-up Pack is only available on Xbox. Anyone playing *Minecraft* on a computer edition can make similar alterations to the look and feel of the game with resource packs. Resource packs can be found and downloaded online at some websites.

CONSOLE COMMANDS

Players of *Minecraft* on the computer and mobile editions also have the ability to alter many aspects of the game using what are

>>*MINECRAFT* ON YOUTUBE

Sports fans have been viewing baseball, football, and basketball on television for decades. Video games have also become a popular spectator sport. Today, many people play and watch competitive gaming, often called e-sports, over the internet. According to Statista, "In 2016, there were 162 million frequent watchers of eSports, with another 131 million who watched occasionally."

Watching other people play *Minecraft* on YouTube has also become extremely popular. *Minecraft* players watch others playing and talking about the game on YouTube, where they can learn tips and tricks, as well as how to create or upload mods. The phenomenon has also become big business and made several YouTube stars very rich just by playing *Minecraft*. Jordan Maron, known by his online username CaptainSparklez, is one of the first YouTubers to become an internet celebrity as a result of his gameplay. CaptainSparklez has ten million subscribers on YouTube, with more than three billion views since he launched in 2010. According to moneynation.com, he has earned millions of dollars from advertisements on his YouTube channel and millions more from the sale of merchandise.

called console commands. Though console commands are easy to use, they fall in between downloadable theme packs and the more complex ability to create or install actual Java mods.

Minecraft console commands are short strings of text, similar to software code, which can be entered inside *Minecraft* while playing. In order to use console commands, a player will need to leave "cheats" turned on before creating a new Minecraft world. A game "cheat" is often a code or setting that allows the player to have an advantage in the game. When the "cheat" setting is on, the player can make customizations to the game.

Here are some examples of how to change the weather in different editions of *Minecraft* using text commands.

- Java Edition: /<weather rain> [1000]
- Pocket Edition: /weather rain 1000

In the Java Edition command, the "less than" and "greater than" symbols—called angle brackets—act as boundaries around fields or directions that are required. In this case, the requirement is that the weather is rainy. The bracket symbols—[and]—indicate an optional field that controls duration of time in seconds. In this case, the duration of rain will be one thousand seconds, or just over sixteen minutes.

Console commands are sometimes referred to as slash commands because they always start with the "/" symbol. Players can learn more about cheats and console commands at minecraft.gamepedia.com and digminecraft.com.

WHAT IS A *MINECRAFT* MOD?

If a player wishes to create *Minecraft* game alterations that cannot be accomplished with resource packs or console commands, he or she can mod some of the *Minecraft* Java code, or write new code from scratch. *Minecraft* mods are more advanced than the simple alterations that console commands can apply to the game.

Mods can add new content to *Minecraft*, alter gameplay, change the way the game looks, and give players more choices in their *Minecraft* world. Some mod changes can be small, such as transforming pigs so they appear like zombie-pigs or skeleton-pigs. Other mod changes can alter the way *Minecraft* is played. One mod called *Thaumcraft* allows a player to become a sorcerer. Another mod called *Aether II: Genesis of the Void* allows players to shoot up into the sky, where they will find giant floating islands.

Creating and installing mods requires additional tools and software, such as the Java Development Kit and *Minecraft* Forge.

JAVA

Making a *Minecraft* mod can be done a few ways. One way is by using the Java software language by coding. The Java software and the Java Development Kit (JDK) are both free to download and use and can be found online at java.com. For anyone who wishes to learn about the basics of coding, Java has dozens of free resources for learning the language.

>>*MINECRAFT* POP CULTURE INVASION

After years on the computer game market, *Minecraft's* popularity only continues to grow. LEGO, action figures, clothing, sleeping bags, mugs, and more are just some of what is available for people who love all things *Minecraft*.

Even CNN news anchor Jake Tapper has a *Minecraft* mug at his desk while he anchors the evening news. When Tapper was asked on Twitter if the mug on his desk was a *Minecraft* coffee mug, he responded, "yes indeed. a Father's Day gift from my creeper-obsessed 4-year-old."

Fans of *Minecraft* have even been able to push for their favorite video game up on the big screen. *Minecraft: The Movie* is set for a release date of May 24, 2019. The film will be directed by Rob McElhenney, with Steve Carell in the starring role. According to CNET.com, the film might be live action and add a new spin to the virtual reality blocky game universe.

>> Award-winning actor Steve Carell is set to star in the big-screen film version of *Minecraft*. Warner Brothers acquired the movie rights for *Minecraft* in 2016. The film is slated for release in 2019.

APIS

Another tool that makes it easier to build mods requires the use of an application programming interface, or API. In computer language, an interface is a device or program that allows two systems to communicate with each other. An API can be used to build mods by allowing the user to write their code directly in the program that will be running it.

One popular API for building *Minecraft* mods is called *Minecraft* Forge and can be found at files.minecraftforge.net. *Minecraft* Forge simplifies installing and switching between mods. Players will need to locate the version of Forge on the website that is compatible with the version of *Minecraft* installed on their computers before downloading it. Players who just want to find mods that have already been created or learn more about mods can look around online and find countless websites with mod libraries and information.

Here is an example of a piece of Java code from the book *Minecraft Modding with Forge: A Family-Friendly Guide to Building Fun Mods in Java.* The code shows how to alter an existing TNT explosion with a fuse in the game to make it bigger. Each line of code is a direction for a different action, motion, or event in the sequence of the blocks, TNT, or explosion.

```
import net.minecraft.entity.Entity;
import net.minecraft.entity.item.EntityItem;
import net.minecraft.entity.item.EntityTNTPrimed;
import net.minecraft.init.Blocks;
import net.minecraft.item.Item;
import net.minecraft.item.ItemStack;
```

```
import net.minecraftforge.event.entity.EntityJoinWorldEvent;
import net.minecraftforge.event.entity.item.ItemExpireEvent;
import net.minecraftforge.fml.common.eventhandler.
SubscribeEvent;

    public class BiggerTNTExplosionsWithFuse {

        int fuse = 4;
        float power = 32.0F;


        @SubscribeEvent
        public void spawn TNTItem(EntityJoinWorldEvent event) {
                if (!(event.entity instanceof EntityTNTPrimed)) {
                        return;
                }
                Entity entity = event.entity;
                EntityItem explosion = new EntityItem(event.world, entity.posX,
                entity.posY, entity.posZ, new ItemStack(Blocks.tnt));
                explosion.setInfinitePickupDelay();
                explosion.motionX = 0;
                explosion.motionY = 0;
                explosion.motionZ = 0;
                explosion.lifespan = fuse * 20;
                if (!event.world.isRemote) {
                        event.world.spawnEntityInWorld(explosion);
                }
        }


        @SubscribeEvent
```

```
public void explode(ItemExpireEvent event) {
        if (event.entityItem.getEntityItem().getItem() != Item
                    .getItemFromBlock(Blocks.tnt)) {
            return;
        }
        EntityItem explosion = event.entityItem;
        event.entity.worldObj.createExplosion(explosion, explosion.posX,
                    explosion.posY, explosion.posZ, power, true);

    }
}
```

The huge block of code written above is named "BiggerTNTExplosionsWithFuse.java." This name tells users what the code is meant to do. The ".java" extension at the end of the file name signifies that it a Java code file.

People who make their own mods are referred to as modders in the *Minecraft* community. Players do not always create their own mods. Many people use mods created by others that have been shared on the internet. Players who want to create their own mods will need to program using Java.

MORE TO KNOW

Computers are not perfect and sometimes they don't work as they are intended. After investing hours or even days creating a world in *Minecraft*, it can be devastating to lose it all after so much effort. There are several ways to keep files safe so that even if a computer breaks, files will remain intact. The simplest way to keep valuable files safe is to make backups each and every time someone finishes a session of *Minecraft*. Once the game has been saved, it is easy to locate the *Minecraft* application and copy it and all associated files to an external hard drive, USB drive, or some other form of storage.

Files can also be backed up on cloud services, which are accessed through the internet. Many companies, including Apple, Google, and Microsoft, offer basic cloud or file backup storage services for free.

Another great way for *Minecraft* players to back up important files is with the use of a *Minecraft* Gameband. The Gameband is a wristband with a built-in flash drive similar to a USB thumb drive. *Minecraft* backups can be stored on the Gameband and taken with players wherever they go.

COMPUTERCRAFT AND BEYOND

ComputerCraft is a very popular mod for *Minecraft* that was created by British game developer Daniel Ratcliffe in 2011. The free downloadable mod allows users to program virtual computers, along with robots called Turtles, within the *Minecraft* world. ComputerCraft uses a scripting programming language called Lua. The name Lua means "moon" in Portuguese, and it is a free language for anyone to use. ComputerCraft is one of the most popular mods ever released for *Minecraft*, and it helped introduce programming to many players.

HOW TO GET STARTED WITH COMPUTERCRAFT

ComputerCraft is a mod for *Minecraft* that allows for computer programming within the game. Players who wish to use this mod and play, program, or experiment with it will need the computer version of *Minecraft* available directly from Mojang.

Minecraft is written with the software language Java, but the ComputerCraft mod allows players to write programs or download existing programs that function within *Minecraft* using the computer language Lua. According to the Lua website, "Lua is a powerful, efficient, lightweight, embeddable scripting language. It supports procedural programming, object-oriented programming, functional programming, data-driven programming, and data description."

Players who wish to learn more about the programming language Lua, which is used for in-game programming with the ComputerCraft mod, can visit www.lua.org. Links to books about programming with the various editions of Lua can be found here: www.lua.org/pil.

Once the *Minecraft* Forge API and the ComputerCraft mod have both been installed, Ratcliffe provides links to YouTube videos that give step-by-step instructions on how to construct a computer and its various components within *Minecraft*. Some of the steps involve taking a resource in the game called cobblestone and fusing it into stone using coal. The resulting stones will be a required resource needed to create a computer with ComputerCraft.

Another step is to use glass blocks to make glass panes. Once all the essential raw materials have been acquired, or crafted, a computer can be built by taking seven stones and surrounding a redstone in the center with a glass pane placed below.

Various other computer components can be made with ComputerCraft, such as a monitor, disc drive, disc, wireless modem, and a printer. Programmable robots made for mining, called Turtles, can also be created with different combinations of raw materials. The computers made and used with the ComputerCraft mod can be programmed to have folders and files

>> Redstone is a resource in *Minecraft* that allows players to create simple electronic connections in the game. It can even be used for computing.

that can be edited, programmed, saved, and even printed—just like a real computer.

HELLO, (COMPUTERCRAFT) WORLD!

"Hello World" is traditionally the first program people write when learning a new programming language. Programmer and author Brian Kernighan created the simple program while he was working at the New Jersey–based research and scientific development company Bell Labs in 1978. The "Hello World" program became famous in a book Kernighan coauthored titled *The C Programing Language*.

The first lesson in the book *The C Programing Language* states the following: "The only way to learn a new programming language is by writing programs in it." The book then goes on to explain, "In C, the program to print "hello, world" is

```
#include <stdio.h>

main( )
{
   printf("hello, world\n");
}
```

The "Hello World" exercise has been used as an introduction to help teach hundreds of software languages. A catalog of the various "Hello World" programs can be found online at helloworldcollection.github.io. The collection has hundreds of "Hello World" programs in various computer languages, in more than seventy spoken languages from around the world.

The first step to make a ComputerCraft "Hello World" program is to type "edit helloworld" into a ComputerCraft computer, which will create and name the new program file that can be edited and saved. To print the words "Hello World" from a ComputerCraft printer, type "print("Hello World!")" then hit the control key on the keyboard and make sure "Save" is selected. Then, press enter. To test it out, type "helloworld" to see if the program is saved and working.

>>COMPUTERCRAFTEDU

Another advancement with the ComputerCaft mods is ComputerCraftEdu. Developed by ComputerCraft's creator, Daniel Ratcliffe, this program helps to teach children computer coding. According to ComputerCraftEdu.com,

> It is a new way to learn computational thinking inside *Minecraft*. Players will start with a tile-based interface

>> Because *Minecraft* can be modified with software code, many kids have been introduced to coding through the game. Online courses help them learn to code from the comfort of their own homes.

to learn the fundamentals of programming in a fun, accessible environment ... Whether you are completely new to programming or you already have some experience, ComputerCraftEdu is an easy and fun way to learn important real world skills and get creative on a whole new level.

ComputerCraftEdu is a mod that focuses on educating its users. It includes a programming environment that uses visual blocks—instead of regular text—to code. Visual programming is very helpful to beginners of any age, because learning an entirely new programming language can take years of practice.

WHAT CAN BE DONE WITH COMPUTERCRAFT?

Minecraft players who want to install and use the ComputerCraft mod can accomplish quite a lot. Players using the mod in *Minecraft* can find and install many existing programs written in the Lua language that are ready for use. There are many locations online to find ComputerCraft programs. The forum section of Daniel Ratcliffe's ComputerCraft website, www.computercraft. info, has a feed dedicated to ComputerCraft Lua programs, with more than four thousand topics listed. There are many categories listed for the various ComputerCraft programs that have been created. A few of them are as follows:

- Turtle programs that utilize the robotlike computers

- Pocket programs that function as small pocket computers
- Command programs that function on command computers, which are powerful versions of advanced ComputerCraft computers
- Games that can be played on the ComputerCraft computer; some of the games available for download are hangman, chess, Connect-4, and Othello

There is even a mod for playing a mini version of *Minecraft* on a ComputerCraft computer within *Minecraft*!

Advanced *Minecraft* players with a knack for programming have taken ComputerCraft into very advanced mods that push the boundaries well beyond what Markus Persson ever imagined for his own game. According to qz.com, or Quartz, "Recent modifications and updates to the game, and unofficial variations created by expert players, such as Tekkit and ComputerCraft, take game functionality to a new level with industrial machines and programmable in-game computers that aren't for entertainment as much as necessary elements to feed Minecrafters' growing appetite for engineering."

MORE MODS TO EXPLORE

The number of *Minecraft* mods that exist is not easy to determine. With so many people online—and no official central database for them—it can be hard to know which mods are worth investigating. Below are two unique mods that players might find interesting.

ScriptCraft is a *Minecraft* server mod created by programmer and writer Walter Higgins. The mod extends *Minecraft* capabilities

```
            $fieldval = 'hidemenu';
            $this->logDocumentChange('hidemenu');
            break;
      case 3:
            $fieldval = 'searchable';
            $this->logDocumentChange('search');
            break;
      case 4:
            $fieldval = 'cacheable';
            $this->logDocumentChange('cache');
            break;                    I
      case 5:
            $fieldval = 'richtext';
            $this->logDocumentChange('richtext');
            break;
      case 6:
            $fieldval = 'deleted';
            $secondaryFields = array (
                'deletedon' => (($_POST['newvalue'] == '1') ? time() : '0'
                'deletedby' => (($_POST['newvalue'] == '1') ? $_SESSION['
            );
            $this->logDocumentChange('delete');
            break;
      default:
            break;
      }
```

>> Though *Minecraft* is written in Java, modders today can use JavaScript—and some clever software tools—to create and modify their favorite game.

using the JavaScript Programming Language. JavaScript should not be confused with Java, despite their similar names.

Higgins wrote a book titled *A Beginner's Guide to Writing Minecraft Plugins in JavaScript*, in which he discusses ScriptCraft. According to Higgins, "ScriptCraft is a plugin for *Minecraft* Servers which lets operators, administrators, and plug-in authors customize the game using JavaScript. ScriptCraft makes it easier to create your own mods." Mods can be written in JavaScript, and the other APIs can be used to run the codes and play the game.

Once installed, ScriptCraft includes a "drone" object that can be used to build complex structures, roads, towns, and even large cities. It also includes many other features that make modding *Minecraft* easier.

OpenComputers is a mod similar to ComputerCraft that adds advanced computers and robots into the *Minecraft* world that can also be programmed using the software language Lua. The difference between OpenComputers and ComputerCraft is that OpenComputers can connect to and interact with the real world outside of the virtual *Minecraft* world. The computers in OpenComputers are also modular, and players using the mod can add additional devices, such as monitors, keyboards, and expansion cards, with capabilities such as graphics and networking. An important in-game device that can be used with this mod is an internet card, which allows players to communicate with the real world through the internet.

According to an article written by Dan Maloney on hackaday.com, "used the OpenComputers mod, which allows placement of programmable in-game computers with a full complement of peripherals, including an Internet connection." The player was then able to "send commands to his ... light bulb—Flip a switch in Minecraft and the real-world light bulb comes on instantly."

THE COMPUTER LANGUAGE BEHIND *MINECRAFT*

While playing a colorful, exciting, and dynamic video game like *Minecraft*, few people consider the computer hardware on which it is running, the software that is powering it, or the many thousands of lines of computer code language that were written to make the game look and behave the way it does. Markus Persson created *Minecraft* with the Java software language. *Minecraft* was released in 2009, but at that point the Java language had already been around for nearly fifteen years. But who created Java and where did it come from?

THE ORIGIN OF JAVA

Steps forward in technology typically build off of innovations and progress that have come before them. The origin of the Java software language began at a computer startup company called Sun Microsystems. Sun Microsystems started as a computer project designed by Stanford University electrical engineering

```
import java.io.*;
import java.net.*;
import java.security.*;

import Protection;

public class Client {
    public void sendAuthentication(String
        Outputstream outstream) throws IOEx
        DataOutputstream out = new DataOutp
        long t1 = (new Date()).getTime();
        double q1 = Math.random();
        byte[] protected1 = Protection.m
        long t2 = (new Date()).getTime(
        double q2 = Math.random();
        byte[] protected2 = Protectior
        out.writeUTF(user);
        out.writeInt(protected1.leng
        out.write(protected2);
        out.flush();
}
}
    public static void main(st
        String host = args[0];
        int port = 7999;
        String user = "John";
        String password = "Sh
        Socket s = new Socke

        Client client = new
            sendAuthent
```

>> The programming language Java was first created so it could be a universal language to run on different software. It is used not only in *Minecraft* but in millions of other applications.

student Andreas Bechtolsheim. While working on his graduate studies at Stanford, Bechtolsheim invented the workstation: an early computer that took an important step away from larger mainframe computers. The workstation would help pave the way for personal computers in the decades that followed. Bechtolsheim, along with Vinod Khosla, Scott McNealy, and Bill Joy, cofounded Sun Microsystems in 1992. The "SUN" part of the name was an acronym for Stanford University Network.

The Java software language started as a secret Sun project originally intended to develop interactive televisions. The Sun Microsystems project was first code-named Stealth before going through various changes as the World Wide Web began to emerge. It was eventually renamed Green, then Oak, and finally Java.

Computer programmer James Gosling, who started working at Sun in 1994, is considered to be the father and creator of Java. Gosling originally wrote the Java language for an early handheld touchscreen device called the Star7, which was being developed by Sun in the early 1990s. The Star7 was never mass-produced, but Gosling and his team created the Java software language to be versatile and run on the Star7 touchscreen as well as a wide variety of different computer systems. The original Java slogan was "write once, run anywhere."

Java was a huge achievement when it was first released in 1995. It was the first universal software language that allowed developers to write applications that could run on any computer. Sun Microsystems was purchased by the software company Oracle for $7.4 billion in 2010.

>>HOW IS JAVASCRIPT DIFFERENT FROM JAVA?

JavaScript is an object-oriented scripting language used to make interactive web pages that often have clickable buttons, animations, and pop-up menus. Brendan Eich created the web programming language in 1995 while he was working at Netscape Communications.

Despite the similarities in name, the Java programming language is different from JavaScript. JavaScript is not part of Java. Unlike Java, JavaScript is not a software language capable of creating independent applications. JavaScript is typically used inside HTML documents and helps to enhance interactive web pages HTML is not capable of producing alone.

ADVANCED JAVA MOD CREATION TOOLS

Learning a software language can seem daunting. With a careful and patient approach, coding in Java to create *Minecraft* mods can be rewarding and fun. Free online tools, such as the Java Development Kit, *Minecraft* Forge, Eclipse, and more, can help ambitious modders take the next steps toward coding.

Below are some necessary *Minecraft* mod creation tools that are needed to code mods with Java. Before downloading files from the internet, make sure to create a new folder on your computer in order to keep everything organized. That will save you a lot of headaches down the line.

JAVA DEVELOPMENT KIT

The first step to writing Java mods for *Minecraft* from scratch is to download the Java Development Kit. This free software comes bundled with the latest version of Java and should be downloaded from the Oracle website. Be sure to check what type of operating system you are using as well (between 32-bit or 64-bit). This will help determine the correct Java Development Kit to download from the Oracle website.

MINECRAFT FORGE

Although there are many tools available to assist with mod building, *Minecraft* Forge is the most popular application loader interface for mod creation. *Minecraft* Forge can be found for free at the *Minecraft* Forge download page: files.Minecraftforge.net. Be sure to check the version of Forge to be sure that it is compatible with the version of *Minecraft* being used before downloading it. If you are not sure, download the recommended version.

ECLIPSE IDE FOR JAVA DEVELOPERS

Another important tool to help with mod creation is an integrated development environment, or IDE. Eclipse is an IDE that can edit, run, and help to correct file errors. Eclipse is a necessary tool for running *Minecraft* to test and edit mod files. Eclipse can be found for free at www.eclipse.org. Be sure to download the version of Eclipse that is compatible with the computer you are using.

NEXT STEPS

The Eclipse IDE for Java Developers is a very useful tool and a good place to get started. After installing Eclipse on your computer, you can launch it and see a welcome screen. This is a great place to begin. Here you will find an overview, tutorials, samples, and more. You can even go through a guided walk-through to create the famous "Hello World" program and begin to familiarize yourself with how Eclipse works and learn what the interface looks like.

MINECRAFT AS EDUCATION

The creative nature of *Minecraft* is why it has become popular with gamers of all ages. Its ability to spark younger players to develop interests with computer coding has many educators considering *Minecraft* as a tool to help teach computer coding at a young age. Teachers, parents, schools, camps, and even governments are all beginning to think of *Minecraft* as much more than just another video game with little to offer beyond being a distraction.

The nonprofit computer science and coding organization Code.org reported that since it partnered with Microsoft in 2015, as many as eighty-five million users have been introduced to the world of computer coding through the game.

Many educators see future benefits for students who pick up basic computer skills, learn to code, and become fluent and familiar with emerging computer technologies. *Minecraft* is bridging the gap between playing and learning and helping students stay engaged with teachers.

MINECRAFT AND PARENTS

Many parents are not familiar with *Minecraft* or how to play it. As a result of this gap in knowledge between parents and kids, there have been many articles and books written specifically for parents in order to help familiarize them with the creative building block game that has been occupying so much of their children's time. *Forbes*, the Huffington Post, the *New York Times*, and Lifehacker.com all have published articles about *Minecraft* for helping parents understand the game.

Parents looking to move their kids away from television and computer screens and into more traditional modes of learning can now offer fans of *Minecraft* several fiction novels that take place in the virtual game world. The novel *Minecraft: The Island* was released in July 2017 by Del Ray and was the first official work of *Minecraft* fiction commissioned by Mojang. The second official *Minecraft* novel, *The Crash*, will be released in July 2018. Mojang also has many other official guidebooks related to learning how to play *Minecraft* as well as advanced play and building techniques.

For parents seeking to involve their kids with computers when school is not in session, the PAST Innovation Lab is one such after-school program that keeps kids having fun while continuing to learn about computer coding, science, and technology. The PAST Foundation was established in 2000 by Annalies Corbin and connects scientific research with classrooms and the public. One of the many after-school programs offered by PAST is a *Minecraft* Mathematics summer program. The course is geared toward students in grades 3 to 5.

Another source for parents related to *Minecraft* is the UK website parentinfo.org, which has several articles dedicated to helping parents of children who play *Minecraft*. One article, titled "Staying Safe on *Minecraft*," answers many common questions parents might have about the game. Another article called "What is *Minecraft?*" introduces the game to parents who may not be familiar with it. There are countless other avenues for involving both kids and parents in learning about computers through *Minecraft*.

MINECRAFTEDU AND TEACHERS AND SCHOOLS

In 2011, Joel Levin, Mikael Uusi-Makela, and Santeri Koivisto began exploring the potential to use video games as a tool to teach. They focused their efforts on *Minecraft* and began a startup company, TeacherGaming, located in Joensuu, Finland. The TeacherGaming mods to alter *Minecraft* into an educational tool became the MinecraftEdu project, which is a modified version of *Minecraft*, to be used by teachers and students. TeacherGaming partnered with Mojang and began licensing MinecraftEdu to schools. By 2016, MinecraftEdu grew in popularity among educators and was being used in more than fifteen thousand schools in more than forty countries around the world.

Microsoft bought Mojang along with *Minecraft* in 2014. After seeing the potential for *Minecraft* as a tool for education, Microsoft acquired MinecraftEdu in 2016 from TeacherGaming for an undisclosed amount of money.

After the purchase, Microsoft and Mojang launched an early access version of MinecraftEdu to teachers and students around the world. In November 2016, the full version of *Minecraft: Education Edition* launched and became available for purchase to anyone online. The MinecraftEdu edition of *Minecraft* is

>> *Minecraft: Education Edition* combines the beloved game with learning. The director of this initiative, Deirdre Quarnstrom, is shown here demonstrating the features of the new edition.

different from the Mojang gaming edition and must be purchased separately. Lessons and lesson plans in math, science, language arts, history, and visual art for different age groups can be found on the MinecraftEdu website.

According to the official education.Minecraft.net website, "Minecraft: Education Edition is a collaborative and versatile platform that educators can use across subjects to encourage 21st-century skills."

>>MINECON

MineCon is an official annual *Minecraft* gaming convention hosted by Mojang. The first MineCon event was held in 2010. The first MineCon convention was called MinecraftCon and was held in Las Vegas, Nevada, to bring fans of *Minecraft* together after the game was first released.

On November 18, 2017, MineCon was video streamed online for free. It was called Minecon EARTH and allowed fans

(continued on the next page)

>> E3, or the Electronic Entertainment Expo, is one of the biggest events in gaming. Excited gamers are shown here playing *Minecraft* at 2017's E3 convention.

(continued from the previous page)

of *Minecraft* who could not attend physically a way to participate virtually. According to the MineCon EARTH website:

> Streamed free worldwide, MINECON Earth was our most global Minecon ever. Will Arnett and Lydia Winters hosted a live show featuring Let's Players, Community Creators, Super (Duper) Musical Numbers, Cosplay Contest Competitors, a Mob Vote that let YOU choose something to be added to *Minecraft*, and Jens' revealing, for the first time ever, the Update Aquatic. It was our biggest Minecon yet, and we couldn't have done it without you. So, thank you!

In an effort to bring the various local *Minecraft* events together, *Minecraft* has now created official *Minecraft* community events. Some of the different partners of the official *Minecraft* community events are Minefaire, MineVention, and Blockfest.

MINECRAFT'S FUTURE IS NOW

Minecraft is having an influence that is generating new games. In 2015, the Department of Education awarded a $900,000 grant to a company called Strange Loop Games that created a game similar to Minecraft called Eco to help teach students about the environment. The game requires that players work together to help avoid an ecological disaster.

According to the Eco website:

Eco is an online game where players must collaborate to build a civilization in a world where everything they do affects the environment. All resources come from a simulated ecosystem, with thousands of plants and animals simulating 24/7. Work together through the player-run government and economy to build the technology to stop a meteor on a collision course with the planet, without polluting the world and killing it off in the process before that even happens.

Various editions of Eco can be purchased online from a single download to classroom editions for up to 100 students.

The future of *Minecraft* can be played right now with the use of virtual reality (VR) headsets. A VR headset allows a *Minecraft* player to be completely immersed into the virtual gaming world and explore and build as if he or she was actually there.

Microsoft encourages interest in STEM (science, technology, engineering, and mathematics) and released new mixed reality (MR) Windows 10 devices for schools. One new chemistry update is planned for the *Minecraft Education Edition*, where teachers can use *Minecraft* to teach students the basics of chemistry.

As gamers, students, parents, and teachers move forward with quickly changing technology, *Minecraft* will play a big part in bridging the gap between gaming and learning in the future.

GLOSSARY

APPLICATION Computer software with a specific purpose, or application, for the user.

APPLICATION LOADER INTERFACE (API) A set of definitions or commands that allow two devices or programs to communicate with each other.

BROWSER A computer application that allows users to access websites on the internet.

CHEATS Methods to change a video game to give the player an advantage or disadvantage beyond the intended gameplay.

COMPATIBLE Able to run or be used on a computer platform, make, or type.

CONSOLE COMMAND Short strings of text, similar to software code, that can be entered inside a game while playing.

DEVELOPER A person who creates software and applications that run on a computer.

GAME CONSOLE A specialized desktop computer system used to play video games.

INTEGRATED DEVELOPMENT ENVIRONMENT (IDE) A compilation of software that combines tools developers need to write and test the software they create.

JAVA Computer language used to write software

MODIFICATION (MOD) A change or alteration in coding to customize how a system works or what it does.

PIXEL The basic unit of programmable elements in a computer display or image.

PLATFORM A computer system made of a hardware device and operating system on which a program runs.

PLUGIN An add-on or extension of a software component that adds a specific feature to its functioning.

SANDBOX GAME A style of video game in which a player can roam in an open virtual world.

SCRIPT A list of commands to be carried out by a programming language.

SLASH COMMANDS Console commands.

SOURCE CODE A text list of commands to be combined or assembled, meant to be run and executed by a computer program.

VIRTUAL REALITY (VR) Computer-generated simulations of 3D environments or images with which a user can seemingly interact.

WORKSTATION Computer terminal meant for technical or scientific work.

Canada Learning Code
129 Spadina Avenue
Toronto, ON M5V2L3
(647) 715-4555
Website: https://www.canadalearningcode.ca
Facebook: @canadalearning code
Instagram and Twitter: @learningcode
Canada Learning Code is an organization dedicated to teaching
   computer coding to all Canadians, focusing especially on
   women, girls, people with disabilities, and
   indigenous peoples.

Code.org
1501 4th Avenue, Suite 900
Seattle, WA 98101
Website: https://code.org
Facebook: @Code.org
Twitter: @codeorg
Code.org is a nonprofit organization that provides access to
   computer science learning in schools, including the
   program Hour of Code.

iD Tech
910 E. Hamilton Avenue, Suite 300
Campell, CA 95008
(888) 709-8324
Website: https://idtech.com
Facebook: @computercamps
Instagram: @idtech

Twitter: @iDTechCamps
iDTech is an organization that runs summer camps for students
   interested in coding.

Kids & Code
320 Catherine Street
Ottawa, ON K1R5T5
(613) 862-1412
Website: http://www.kidsandcode.org
Kids & Code is a Canada-based organization dedicated to
   offering classes, workshops, and events for kids interested
   in learning to code.

Kids Code Jeunesse
51 Sherbrooke Ouest, #6
Montreal, Quebec H2X1X2
Website: http://kidscodejeunesse.org
Facebook: @KidsCodeJeunesse
Twitter: @KidsCoding
Kids Code Jeunesse is an organization dedicated to teaching
   Canadian children to code through workshops in schools,
   libraries, and community centers.

MVCode Clubs
3236 Geary Boulevard
San Francisco, CA
(415) 569-2112
Website: https://www.mvcodeclub.com
Facebook, Instagram, and Twitter: @mvcodeclub

MVCode Clubs provide summer camps and after-school programs for students who want to learn to code.

Tynker Coding for Kids
4410 El Camino Real, Suite 104
Los Altos, CA 94022
Website: https://www.tynker.com
Facebook: @Gotynker
Instagram: @tynkercoding
Twitter: @gotynker
Tynker is a company that provides coding and technology programs for children interested in computer sciences.

FOR FURTHER READING

Ab, Mojang. *Minecraft: Guide to Creative.* New York, NY: Del Rey, 2017.

Conrod, Philip. *Java for Kids: NetBeans 8 Programming Tutorial.* Kidware Software, 2017.

Foster, Stephen, Sarah Guthals, and Lindsay Handley. *Minecraft Modding for Kids for Dummies.* Seattle, WA: Amazon Digital Services, LLC, 2015.

Garcia, Nadia Ameziane. *Java for Kids (and Grown-Ups): Learn to Code and Create Your Own Projects with Java 8.* Seattle, WA: Amazon Digital Services, LLC, 2017.

Gupta, Arun. *Minecraft Modding with Forge: A Family-Friendly Guide to Building Fun Mods in Java.* Seattle, WA: O'Reilly Media, 2015.

Higgins, Walter. *A Beginner's Guide to Writing Minecraft Plugins in JavaScript.* San Francisco, CA: Peachpit Press, 2015.

Miller, John. *Unofficial Minecraft Lab for Kids: Family-Friendly Projects for Exploring and Teaching Math, Science, History, and Culture Through Creative Building.* Seattle, WA: Amazon Digital Services, LLC, 2016.

Miller, Megan. *Hacks for Minecrafters: Mods: The Unofficial Guide to Tips and Tricks That Other Guides Won't Teach You.* Seattle, WA: Amazon Digital Services, LLC, 2016.

Miller, Megan. *The Ultimate Unofficial Encyclopedia for Minecrafters: An A–Z Book of Tips and Tricks the Official Guides Don't Teach You.* Seattle, WA: Sky Pony Press, 2015.

Richardson, Craig, *Learn to Program with Minecraft: Transform Your World with the Power of Python.* New York, NY: Penguin Random House Publishers Services, 2015.

Thompson, Chandler R. *Java Programming for Kids: Learn Java Step by Step and Build Your Own Interactive Calculator for Fun!* Seattle, WA: Amazon Digital Services, LLC, 2014.

Bloomberg.com. "Brian W. Kernighan." Retrieved April 7, 2018. https://www.bloomberg.com/research/stocks/private /person.asp?personId=30218371&privcapId =7505588&previousCapId=7505588&previousTitle =Elemental%2520Cyber%2520Security,%2520Inc.

Cheshire, Tom. "Changing the Game: How Notch Made *Minecraft* a Cult Hit." Wired.com, September 15, 2014. http://www.wired.co.uk/article/changing-the-game.

Johnson, Ben. "Microsoft Buys MinecraftEdu, plans edition for schools." Marketplace.org, January 20, 2016. https://www .marketplace.org/2016/01/20/tech /microsoft-buys-minecraftedu-plans-edition-schools.

Mac, Ryan. "Inside the Post-Minecraft Life of Billionaire Gamer God Markus Persson." *Forbes*, March 3, 2015. https://www.forbes.com/sites/ryanmac/2015/03/03 /minecraft-markus-persson-life-after-microsoft -sale/#419249691616.

Maloney, Dan. "The Internet of *Minecraft* Things is Born." Hackaday.com, November 25, 2015. https://hackaday .com/2015/11/25/the-internet-of-minecraft-things-is-born.

Ovide, Shira, and Evelyn M. Rusli. "Microsoft Gets 'Minecraft'—Not the Founders." *Wall Street Journal*, September 15, 2014. https://www.wsj.com/articles /microsoft-agrees-to-acquire-creator-of-minecraft -1410786190.

Peckham, Matt. "Check Out How Insanely Big This New Lego *Minecraft* Set Is." Time.com, May 18, 2017. http://time .com/4782917/lego-minecraft-mountain-cave-biggest.

Peterson, Andrea. "The Government is Helping Fund a *Minecraft*-Style Game for Teaching Kids About the Environment." *Washington Post*, June 9, 2015. https://www.washingtonpost.com/news/the-switch/wp/2015/06/09/the-government-is-helping-fund-a-minecraft-style-game-for-teaching-kids-about-the-environment/?utm_term=.5c68772b78d2.

Rahming, A. K. "Over 144 Million Copies of Minecraft Have Been Sold So Far." X-Box Enthusiast.com, January 22, 2018. http://xboxenthusiast.com/2018/01/22/144-million-copies-minecraft-sold-far.

Robertson, Andy. "What Parents Need to know About '*Minecraft*' Better Together." Forbes.com, September 13, 2017. https://www.forbes.com/sites/andyrobertson/2017/09/13/what-parents-need-to-know-about-minecraft-better-together/#1c293cccbf91.

Stuart, Keith. "Minecraft Free for Every Secondary School in Northern Ireland." *Guardian*, March 25, 2015. https://www.theguardian.com/technology/2015/mar/25/minecraft-free-secondary-school-northern-island.

Thompson, Clive. "The Minecraft Generation: How a clunky Swedish computer game is teaching millions of children to master the digital world." *New York Times*, April 14, 2016. https://www.nytimes.com/2016/04/17/magazine/-minecraft-generation.html.

Twistedsifter.com. "Artists Gives Real-Life Animals the *Minecraft* Treatment." May 9, 2017. http://twistedsifter.com/2017/05/artists-gives-real-life-animals-the-minecraft-treatment.

Vrabel, Jeff. "Why do my kids waste hours watching millennials play video games on YouTube?" *Washington Post*, October 12, 2017. https://www.washingtonpost.com/news/parenting/wp/2017/10/12/why-do-my-kids-waste-hours-watching-millennials-play-video-games-on-youtube/?utm_term=.9d9ee64f2820.

Ward, Mark. "Why *Minecraft* is more than just another video game." BBC.com, September 7, 2013. http://www.bbc.com/news/magazine-23572742.

Wingfield, Nick, and Natasha Singer. "*Minecraft* Acquires Minecraft App for Schools." *New York Times*, January 19, 2016. https://www.nytimes.com/2016/01/20/technology/microsoft-acquires-minecraftedu-tailored-for-schools.html.

INDEX

A

application programming interface (API), 26, 37

B

blocks, 4, 9, 13, 14, 15, 31

C

Code.org, 45
computer code, 4, 5, 7, 17, 22, 26, 28, 37, 39
ComputerCraft, 30–32, 33, 34, 35, 36
  ComputerCraftEdu, 34–35
  Turtles, 30, 31, 35
computer software, 4, 16, 17, 39
  application software, 16
  system software, 16
console commands, 20–21, 22
creepers, 9, 13

E

Eclipse IDE for Java Developers, 42, 43, 44
education, 35, 45, 46, 47, 48, 50–51
  Eco, 50–51
  e-sports, 21
  parents, 45–47, 51
  schools, 45, 47, 48, 51

G

Gameband, 29
game consoles, 7, 10, 19, 20
  PlayStation, 10, 19, 20
  Xbox, 10, 19, 20
game modes, 4, 12
  adventure, 12, 14
  creative, 12, 13, 14
  hardcore, 12, 14
  spectator, 12, 14
  survival, 12, 13, 14
gameplay, 12, 13, 18, 23

H

"Hello World," 32–33, 44
Higgins, Walter, 36, 37
  Beginner's Guide to Writing Minecraft Plugins in JavaScript, A, 37

I

integrated development environment (IDE), 43

J

Java, 7, 16, 17, 20, 21, 22, 24, 26, 28, 30, 37, 39, 41, 42, 43
  Gosling, James, 41
  Sun Microsystems, 39, 41
Java Development Kit (JDK), 24, 42, 43
JavaScript, 37, 42
  Eich, Brendan, 42

K

Kernighan, Brian, 32–33
  C Programing Language, The, 33

L

LEGO, 10, 15, 24
  sets, 15–16
Lua, 30, 31, 35, 38

M

mash-up packs, 20
Microsoft, 6, 12, 18, 45, 47, 51
MineCon, 49–50
Minecraft Forge, 24, 26, 31, 42, 43
Minecraft Modding with Forge, 17, 26
mobile devices, 7, 10, 19
mobs, 10
mods, 4, 18, 22, 23, 24, 26, 28, 30, 35, 36, 37, 42
Mojang, 6, 10, 12, 15, 18, 30, 47, 49
  sale of, 6, 12, 47

O

online gaming, 12
OpenComputers, 38

P

personal computers, 7, 10, 19
Persson, Markus "Notch," 5–6, 9, 10–12, 15, 16, 36, 39
  career, 6, 11–12
  influences, 10–11, 15
  story, 5–6, 10–11
pop culture, 24
popularity, 4, 12

Porser, Jakob, 12
programmers, 16, 17

R

Ratcliffe, Daniel, 30, 31, 34, 35
release date, 6, 12
resource packs, 20

S

sales figures, 4, 6, 7, 12
sandbox game, 9
saving work, 28–29
ScriptCraft, 36–37, 38
single player, 12
skin packs, 20

T

TeacherGaming, 47
  MinecraftEdu, 47–48
texture packs, 9, 20
theme packs, 20

U

updates, 6–7, 18

Y

YouTube, 21, 31

ABOUT THE AUTHOR

Adam Furgang was fortunate enough to be raised in the 1970s, the golden age of gaming. He was among the first generation of kids to play video games at home. He has over three decades of experience playing video games, Dungeons & Dragons, and numerous other tabletop role-playing and board games. He continues to play games of all types, including *Minecraft*, with his two sons and runs a blog, wizardsneverweararmor.com, that concentrates on gaming, art, and films.

PHOTO CREDITS

Cover michaeljung/Shutterstock.com; cover, back cover, pp. 1, 4–5 (background) © iStockphoto.com/letoakin; p. 5 Bloomberg /Getty Images; pp. 6, 32 Karen Huang; p. 8 PA Images /Alamy Stock Photo; p. 9 urbanbuzz/Shutterstock.com; p. 11 Radharc Images/Alamy Stock Photo; p. 15 patat /Shutterstock.com; p. 18 Future Publishing/Getty Images; p. 19 OlegDoroshin/Shutterstock.com; p. 23 theodore liasi /Alamy Stock Photo; p. 25 J. Kempin/Getty Images; p. 34 Imgorthand/E+/Getty Images; p. 37 ar4baldo/Shutterstock.com; p. 40 kr7sztof/E+/Getty Images; p. 48 Andrew Kelly/AP Images for Microsoft; p. 49 Mark Ralston/AFP/Getty Images.

Design and Layout: Nicole Russo-Duca; Editor: Siyavush Saidian; Photo Researcher: Karen Huang